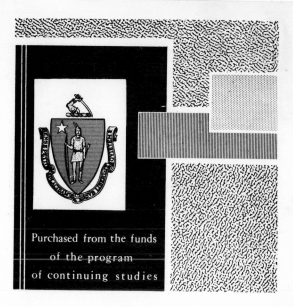

Evelyn Waugh

by CHRISTOPHER HOLLIS

Published for the British Council
and the National Book League
by Longmans, Green & Co

Two shillings and sixpence net

Evelyn Waugh established his reputation as one of our leading novelists with his first novel, *Decline and Fall*, published in 1928. He has maintained this reputation and has continued to portray and satirize, with brilliant comic invention, the upper-class society of his own generation. Mr. Hollis, in this sympathetic appreciation, suggests that Evelyn Waugh's study of the Catholic martyr, Edmund Campion, marked a turning-point in his literary development; from this study he learned the sundering nature of the Church's claims, and in his later novels he examines the effect of these claims on the Catholic living in modern, irreligious society. For this revised edition Mr. Hollis has included a consideration of Evelyn Waugh's most recent works.

Mr. Hollis has written a number of books, including several on literary subjects, an analysis of economic problems, and *Death of a Gentleman*, published in 1943. His essay on G. K. Chesterton appears in this series. He is a director of the publishing firm of Hollis and Carter and a member of the Table of Punch. He was a Member of Parliament for ten years.

Bibliographical Series
of Supplements to 'British Book News'
on Writers and *Their Work*

GENERAL EDITOR
Geoffrey Bullough

EVELYN WAUGH

Mark Gerson

EVELYN WAUGH

by

CHRISTOPHER HOLLIS

PUBLISHED FOR
THE BRITISH COUNCIL
AND THE NATIONAL BOOK LEAGUE
BY LONGMANS, GREEN & CO

LONGMANS, GREEN & CO LTD
48 Grosvenor Street, London W.1

*Associated companies, branches and
representatives throughout the world*

First published 1954
Revised editions 1958, 1966
Revised edition © Christopher Hollis 1966

*Printed in Great Britain by
F. Mildner & Sons, London, E.C.1*

EVELYN WAUGH

WITH his first novel, *Decline and Fall*, published in 1928, Mr. Evelyn Waugh established his reputation as the novelist of the Bright Young Things of the 1920's. He established himself thus at one bound as one of the leading novelists of the day, and has since maintained that reputation. At the same time his talent, like that of other novelists, has developed over the years and he has perhaps sometimes had a little difficulty in persuading his admirers to keep pace with his development.

Mr. Evelyn Waugh recently prophesied that in the coming years he would find in himself a growing interest in literary form and growing interest in religion, and he added the further prophecy that a world which in its decline was returning to its catacombs would pay less and less attention to such interests. Whether his pessimism about the trend of the world was justified, this is not the place to consider, but the two tests to which Mr. Waugh submits himself are the two tests which are pertinent as much for his past as for his future work.

Mr. Waugh's characterization is often criticized on grounds that show, I think, a misunderstanding of his intentions. He has sometimes been criticized for his lack of pity, but the criticism, I think, a little misses the point. It may indeed fairly be said of his earlier works that, brilliant and funny as they are, they give us a picture of a society of irremediable futility. There is obvious sincerity in incidental remarks, such as that put into the mouth of Adam Symes, in *Vile Bodies*, that such futility must inevitably be leading to catastrophe, and there is an artistic wit in the conclusion of *Vile Bodies* which tells us of the coming of another world war without bothering even to answer the quite secondary question between whom the war is fought.

Yet, if we turn from the portrait of society at large to the portrait of individuals, the criticism of lack of pity has little meaning. For the characters in his first two novels, *Decline and Fall* and *Vile Bodies*, are too wholly fantastic for any question of sympathy or antipathy to arise. No one can shed tears over the death of Mr. Prendergast or of Agatha Runcible because they are clearly not real people. In the work on which he was engaged when the war broke out and which he published in its uncompleted form, under the title of *Work Suspended*, Mr. Waugh puts into the mouth of John Plant, the detective story novelist, a description of what is essentially, at least in his earlier books, his own attitude towards his characters.

The algebra of fiction must reduce its problems to symbols if they are to be soluble at all. I am shy of a book commended to me on the grounds that the 'characters are alive'. There is no place in literature for a live man, solid and active. At best the author may maintain a kind of Dickensian menagerie, where his characters live behind bars, in darkness, to be liberated twice nightly for a brief gambol under the arc lamps: in they come to the whip crack, dazzled, deafened, and doped, tumble through their tricks and scamper out again, to the cages behind which the real business of life, eating and mating, is carried on out of sight of the audience. 'Are the lions really alive?' 'Yes, lovey.' 'Will they eat us up?' 'No lovey, the man won't let them'—that is all the reviewers means as a rule when they talk of 'life'. The alternative, classical expedient is to take the whole man and reduce him to a manageable abstraction. Set up your picture plain, fix your point of vision, make your figure twenty foot high or the size of a thumb-nail, he will be life-size on your canvas; hang your picture in the darkest corner, your heaven will still be its one source of light. Beyond these limits lie only the real trouser buttons and the *crêpe* hair with which the futurists used to adorn their paintings.

It is a different story when we move on to the third and fourth novels, *Black Mischief* and *A Handful of Dust*. *A Handful of Dust* is, from this point of view, a transitional novel. It is quite easy to believe that Tony Last might have perished in the Guiana jungle or might have been kept there in some perpetual captivity. It is hard to believe in the reality of his condemnation to the perpetual reading of Dickens to the mad Mr. Todd. It is true that, if we may judge from Mr. Waugh's atobiographical *Ninety-two Days*, Mr. Todd owed some of his characteristics to the real Mr. Christie, whom Mr. Waugh met in the Guianan jungle, and that he owed his fondness for Dickens to Father Mather, a very different sort of man in every other way, who also inhabited that part of the world. But reality is in the novel deliberately transformed into unreality. This is amusing but not real. On the other hand, all the early part of the book is very real. We can feel sorrow for the death of young John Last, as we cannot feel it for Agatha Runcible and Mr. Prendergast. We can hate the self-deceiving, heartless selfishness of Brenda and can pity the stupid, wooden goodness of Tony.

But it is not until we come to *Brideshead Revisited* that we come to what may be called a wholly three-dimensional novel—to a novel on whose characters we can pass judgements as if they were real people.

On the other hand, that is by no means to say that the early novels can fairly be dismissed as merely frivolous, nor even that the religious influences which have been so predominant in Mr. Waugh's later work were wholly absent even then. In *Vile Bodies*, the whole point of the character of Mrs. Ape—a sort of twentieth-century Sludge—is that, with all the absurdity and vulgarity of her commercial evangelism, she does in the last resort believe in her own gospel and in the reality of a hell-fire for 'angels' who go wrong.

In this novel, too, we get the appearance of the Jesuit, Father Rothschild. Mr. Waugh would, I think, be the first to admit that he knows a great deal more about Jesuits today than he did then. As a matter of incidental fact, of course, no Jew could then be a Jesuit, and in any event nothing is more wildly improbable of any Jesuit of twentieth-century England than that he would have an uncanny knowledge of everybody's secrets or be engaged in confidential conclaves with the Prime Minister. Yet, if Mr. Waugh at that time knew very little of what a Jesuit would be expected to say in detail, the part assigned to Father Rothschild in the novel shows clearly that he was beginning to feel that here were men who had something to say which the follies of the world neglected at their peril—here were men who had a secret, if only one could discover what it was.

These two novels—*Decline and Fall* and *Vile Bodies*—were the novels which Mr. Waugh wrote before he became a Catholic. But that does not mean that the hints which are to be found in Father Rothschild are at once followed up in his succeeding work immediately after his reception. Just to the contrary. From this point of view, Mr. Waugh's work falls rather into three periods, and immediately after his reception—in the second period—in his novels, *A Handful of Dust* and *Black Mischief*, there are, it is true, many parodies of the habits of Eastern Schismatics, and the Catholic missionary at Marodi in *Black Mischief* is the only one who keeps his head when the army is expected, but in general there is less direct reference than in any of his works earlier or later, to religion, Tony Last, in *A Handful of Dust*, goes, it is true, regularly to his village church, but that it was a social rather than a religious sense which took him there is amply proved by his frank admission to Mr. Todd at the end of the book that he had never considered whether he believed in God. For anything like a Catholic work of fiction in this period we must go to his short story *Out of Depth*, in which a worldly and foolish Catholic American man of fashion is transported by a magician into a future age, in which the blacks are the master and the whites the subject race, in which the only survival of a wholly changed society which he can recognize as familiar is the survival of the Mass.

Black Mischief is the study of the politics of an Abyssinia-like African island whose Emperor Seth attempts to impose on his barbarous subjects what he conceives to be the customs of 'modern progress', and the story is enlivened by the sub-plots of the absurd French Minister's suspicions of the yet more absurd British Minister, and the antics of two ridiculous British spinsters who arrive at Debra Dowa, Azania's capital. The book has been strangely and perversely misunderstood. Some critics have deduced from Mr. Waugh's mockery of Seth that he is unsympathetic to African self-government, others from his mockery of Dame Mildred Porch and Miss Tin that he is sympathetic to cruelty to animals. Others, more strangely still, have condemned his Pageant of Birth Control on the ground that the description of it will in some way favour the cause of birth control. Whatever may be Mr. Waugh's opinions on African self-government or on cruelty to animals, they cannot fairly be deduced from this book. All that is here satirized and attacked is insincerity. The reasons for Seth's absurdity and failure are that what he is importing into Azania in the name of Western progress is not Western progress at all but merely the catchwords of some of its silliest fashions, that Seth uses the language of progress but he uses the methods of barbarism, that his people are wholly barbaric and whatever merits European ways may have in Europe they are meaningless among the savages of Azania. Seth had brought back from Europe no understanding of anything but its absurdities. Professor Toynbee in our own days has told us how much easier it is to spread rapidly the superficial techniques of European civilization than it is to spread its spiritual essence—and how much more dangerous —and the evidence of this danger we can see clearly around us. Mr. Waugh said it all a great deal more amusingly than Professor Toynbee, and twenty years before him.

So, too, the issue raised by Dame Mildred Porch and Miss Tin is not in the least the issue whether it is good or bad to be kind to animals. Again it is an issue of simple sincerity. The indictment against the two ladies is merely that they are selfish frauds. They have not taken the trouble to find out how, if at all, they can benefit animals. They never do the smallest good to any animal. On the other hand, with their selfish thoughtlessness they give a great deal of trouble to a great many human beings.

Mr. Waugh's characters can, as has been said, be divided into those in whose reality we can believe and those in whose reality we cannot believe. For the most part the characters in *Black Mischief* are of the second sort. Mr. Youkhoumian, for instance, is a good example of what is meant by an unreal character. If anyone was so priggish as to sit in solemn judgement on Mr. Youkhoumian as if he were a person in real life, it would be necessray to condemn him as a most thorough-faced villain, an unsatisfactory citizen. To have dealings with such an unflagging cheat in flesh and blood would be wholly tiresome. But, in print, he is indeed sufficiently unreal for us not greatly to care what happens to him. His survival is artistically justified as a symbol that in such societies as those of Azania, trickery and dishonesty will finally triumph whatever the changes of regime. Yet few readers' tears would have been shed if he had come to a bad end. In print we can afford to like him for the quaintness of his conversation. It is a luxury that we could not afford in the flesh. We cannot shed many tears over the various Azanians from Seth downwards who come to bloody ends, because we have never been shown in them sufficient human emotion for us to feel them to be human beings. But Prudence, the British Envoy Extraordinary's silly little daughter, with her absurd Panorama of Life and her affairs first with William and then with Basil Seal, is a little different. She is real, if ridiculous.

'You're a grand girl, Prudence, and I'd like to eat you', says Basil Seal. 'So you shall, my sweet . . . anything you want', answers Prudence.

It is a somewhat forced and unnatural phrase of compliment in itself, and is only brought in to give point to the horrible *dénouement* when Basil Seal at the end of the book finds that he has been entertained unaware on the flesh of Prudence by his barbaric hosts of Moshu at Seth's funeral feast. It could indeed be argued that no way could be found of more powerfully exposing the absurdity of Seth's ambition to modernize Azania, but the incident is a little too horrible for the stomach to take.

But it is in the third period—the period in which he still lives—rather than in the second, to which we can, I think, look for a conscious and deliberate use of his powers for a study of religious problems. And, in so far as we can ascribe that development to an influence derived from his own writing, that influence was, I think, quite certainly his study of the Elizabethan Jesuit martyr, Edmund Campion, which he published in 1935—Edmund Campion, one of the great masters of prose in his day, a man to whom a brilliant career in the world lay open. After hesitation he rejected all compromise and decided that no solution was tolerable save that of total surrender to the claims of the Church. 'Surely it was not expected of him to give up *all*?' wrote Mr. Waugh in rhetorical question.

Mr. Waugh twice visited Abyssinia as a newspaper correspondent. The first visit was in 1930, when Abyssinia was not yet much in the public eye, to report on the coronation of Haile Selassie as Emperor. The second visit was as a war correspondent at the time of the Italo-Abyssinian War in 1935. Each visit was followed by a book of travel reminiscence—*Remote People* from the first visit, and *Waugh on Abyssinia* from the second. Mr. Waugh at that time welcomed the overthrow of Selassie's regime by the Italians and hoped that the new regime would bring a decent European influence into the land. Each of these two books was followed by a novel—*Black Mischief* followed the first, and *Scoop* the second. The nominal scene of the first novel, as has been said, is the island of Azania off the African coast; of the second, Ishmaelia on the mainland. Azania is under the rule of the Emperor Seth, Ishmaelia under a normal Republic which is managed by the Negro family of Jackson. Azania is troubled by the reforming and modernizing ambitions of its own Emperor, but recently returned from Oxford University. In Ishmaelia the Jacksons are themselves innocent of progressive ambitions. There the disruptive influences are those of white concession-hunters, attracted by the country's mineral wealth. Russians and Germans intrigue against one another and plunge the country—or at least the capital—into revolution. Both are in the end defeated by a mysterious Mr. Baldwin, who arrives in a helicopter, speaks all languages, captures all power, proclaims himself a British subject, and is, in general, very much the sort of character that Disraeli might have put into a novel if only Disraeli had made his jokes on purpose.

Yet *Scoop* is by no means a repetition of *Black Mischief* with a few details different. It is a study of what is to some extent the same problem from an opposite end. *Black Mischief* was concerned with how Africans behave when they come in contact with the superficial patter of European culture. *Scoop* is concerned with how Europeans, who know nothing of their culture except its superficial patter, make use of Africans for their absurd purposes. *Scoop* is concerned with the popular Press—with showing how the Press exploits a 'story' of the troubles of this African Republic, which neither its readers nor its writers remotely attempt to understand, to provide for a few days the inane sensationalism that it needs for its own continuance. Europe's invasion of Africa in *Scoop* is a tragic futility because it is merely the scum of Europe which is settling upon the scum of Africa—because it is the least estimable and most ephemeral aspect of European culture which is settling itself upon Africa. Africa's imitation of Europe in *Black Mischief* is similarly cursed. But Mr. Waugh's visit to the Abyssinia monastery of Debra Lebanos, which he describes in *Remote People*, shows him another plane on which West and East meet one another, of which it would have been out of place to have written in those two satirical novels—the plane on which the West really is the liberator of the East.

I had sometimes thought it an odd thing that Western Christianity, alone of all the religions of the world, exposes its mysteries to every observer, but I was so accustomed to this openness that I had never before questioned whether it was an essential and natural feature of the Christian system. Indeed, so saturated are we in this spirit that many people regard the growth of the Church as a process of elaboration, even of obfuscation; they visualize the Church of the first century as a little cluster of pious people reading the Gospels together, praying and admonishing each other with a simplicity to which the high ceremonies and subtle theology of later years would have been bewildering and unrecognizable. At Debra Lebanos I suddenly saw the classic basilica and open altar as a great positive achievement, a triumph of light over darkness consciouly accomplished, and I saw theology as the science of simplification by which nebulous and elusive ideas are formalized and made intelligible and exact. I saw the Church of the first century as a dark and hidden thing; as dark and hidden as the seed germinating in the womb; legionaries off duty slipping furtively out of barracks, greeting each other by signs and passwords in a locked upper room in the side street of some Mediterranean seaport; slaves at dawn creeping from the grey twilight into the candle-lit, smoky chapels of the catacombs. The priests hid their office, practising trades; their identity was known only to initiates, they were criminals against the law of their country. And the pure nucleus of the truth lay in the minds of the people, encumbered with superstitions, gross survivals of the paganism in which they had been brought up; hazy and obscene nonsense seeping through from the other esoteric cults of the Near East, magical infections from the conquered barbarian. And I began to see how these obscure sanctuaries had grown, with the clarity of the Western reason, into the great open altars of Catholic Europe, where Mass is said in a flood of light, high in the sight of all, while tourists can clatter round with their Baedekers, incurious of the mystery.

In *Scoop* Lord Copper, the newspaper magnate, proprietor of the *Daily Beast*, is asked by a society hostess, as a favour, to send out to Ishmaelia as correspondent a young literary protégé of hers, a Mr. Boot. Through an absurd muddle in the *Beast* office, a namesake of his, another Boot, the paper's nature correspondent, is sent out instead. He is utterly unsuited for the job, and at first proves himself wholly incompetent, and is indeed dismissed by his newspaper. But then, by obstinately remaining in the capital, at a time when the revolutionary Mr. Benito had sent all the other correspondents out into the country on a wild-goose chase, solely

that they might be out of the way when the revolution
started, he stumbles on news of sensational interest which
Mr. Baldwin enables him to exploit. He returns to England
to find himself hailed as the greatest of war correspondents
and Lord Copper plans for him a knighthood—though by
another muddle the knighthood is actually given to another
Boot.

All this is most excellent fooling, and Mr. Waugh is very
careful in this book not to mix his fooling with anything
that could shock either a moral or an aesthetic susceptibility.
There is much comic squalor but no story of any atrocity
to any of the characters in the book. There is no talk of
religion one way or the other. Except for one incident
between Boot and a German girl, there is no sex in the book.
Its purpose is quite clearly that of a criticism of the veil of a
popular newspaper—for destroying by its attacks on all
quiet living all relics of those traditions of our civilization
in their readers.

The coming of the war found Mr. Waugh at work on a
novel of the inter-war society. That society, Mr. Waugh
felt, was irretrievably shattered by September 1939.
Neither had he the will to complete the book, nor did the
world exist to receive it. Nevertheless, so far as it went,
the work pleased him above any of its predecessors. He
therefore published the two episodes of it which he had
completed—that of the death of John Plant's father and of
John's relations with Lucy Simmonds—by themselves,
under the title of *Work Suspended*. He dedicated this frag-
ment to Alexander Woollcott in a letter, in which he wrote,
'So far as it went, this was my best writing.'

Whether it would have been Mr. Waugh's best book, he
can perhaps judge, but we certainly cannot, for he knows
how the full unity would have shaped itself, where we can
only guess. But certainly he gives us here a sustained
excellence of style, which we are to get again in *Brideshead
Revisited*, but which we had not found in the earlier books.
We are no longer in the world of the jerky, short, comic

sentences of conversation, and, although it is from *Work Suspended* that the passage comes that has already been quoted, in which John Plant rejects the obligation on the novelist to give a picture of a 'full' man, in fact John Plant's description of the method of the novelist applies much more nearly to Mr. Waugh's methods in his earlier books than in this. For all Plant's protestation that he will not give the reader a description of his love for Lucy, there is every indication that he would have done so had the book gone on much longer. The book is the forerunner of *Brideshead Revisited* in the sense that its characters are much more nearly full and real people than those of the preceding books. John Plant, in the course of the book, explains to his publisher, Mr. Bennell, that he feels that he has now mastered the technique of the detective novel and that he must move on to the solution of other problems. Mr. Waugh himself seems in the same way to have come with this work to the feeling that a mere repetition of his previous work would be profitless and that the time had come for the mastery of a new form.

During the war Mr. Waugh occupied a period of mounting guard on Italian prisoners in a troopship in writing *Put Out More Flags*. A book about the war, written during the war by a serving soldier, it is a book written under a handicap. As he was later to show in *Men At Arms*, Mr. Waugh was as capable of satirizing the foibles of serving soldiers as of Bright Young People, but neither good taste nor King's Regulations would permit at the moment of our peril the saying of a number of things which could well be said in easier times. The book is dedicated to Mr. Randolph Churchill and concerns itself, as the dedicatory letter explains, with that 'odd, dead period before the Churchillian Renaissance'.

'There's a new spirit abroad,' says the absurd Sir Joseph Mainwaring in the closing sentences of the book. 'I see it on every side.'

'And,' adds Mr. Waugh, 'poor booby, he was right.'

The bulk of the novel is concerned with Basil Seal's attempt to extract profit and amusement out of the war—profit by hawking round the countryside an impossibly odious family of slum children, called the Connollies, billeting them on unoffending householders and then taking money to remove them elsewhere; amusement, by tricking his friend, Ambrose Silk, into writing what might pass for a Fascist pamphlet and then denouncing him. As a foil to Basil Seal, Mr. Waugh has to show us examples of characters—Freddy Sothill, Alastair Trumpington, Cedric Lyme—quietly joining up and behaving admirably—in the case of Cedric, getting killed in Norway. Alastair Trumpington is an important character in Mr. Waugh's world and indeed in the world in general. He stands between the Seals and the Flytes. He is not of the company to whom the language of religion is familiar, nor, having forgotten religion, has he, like Basil Seal, forgotten all decency of conduct. A 'socialite', as it is now called, he has perhaps no principles in the strict intellectual sense, but, while passing no judgement on others who do not share his prejudices, he finds within himself things that he would prefer to do and not to do. He likes to fight for his country when she is at war, just as he likes to wear the sort of hat that the convention of society demands for the season of the year. He likes to fight for his country, and an emotion which one can call equally patriotism or masochism makes him like to punish himself by fighting in a peculiarly unpleasant and a peculiarly dangerous manner—first in the ranks and then in the commandos. Mr. Waugh puts before us the reminder that there is this kind of irreligious virtue to be found in the world, and leaves us to wonder whether in the world of Basil Seal it is likely to be sufficiently strong, and whether in the world of Miles Plastic it is likely to survive. We are indeed left at the end of *Put Out More Flags* with a vague impression that in the new atmosphere of the Churchillian Renaissance even Basil Seal is going to behave decently. There is some admirable fooling at the expense of the

Ministry of Information, which is most amusing. But Basil Seal's antics—his dodge of selling the Connollies—though ingenious, is not, to tell the truth, especially amusing. It is a little bit the kind of thing that curates do in novels by George A. Birmingham. The trouble with Basil Seal is that, if we consider him a real character, he is too odious to be funny. Had he been content to remain a character in one of Mr. Waugh's earlier novels, such as *Decline and Fall*—in a fantastic world of fantastic people—we could have laughed at him as a mere formula of villainy without any attempt to pass a moral judgement on a person. We can tolerate him even in Azania. But in a real world, alongside real and suffering people at a great crisis of our history, he is too horrible.

Brideshead Revisited is the story of an officer serving in the war, Charles Ryder, whose military duties bring him by accident to the country house of Brideshead. Brideshead is the home of the Flyte family, an old Catholic family, with whose life Charles Ryder had been curiously intermixed in the old days before the war. First, as an undergraduate, he had had a too intimate friendship at Oxford with the younger son of the family, Sebastian Flyte, and then later, when he had won himself a certain position in life as an artist, he had had an affair with Sebastian's sister, Julia.

With *Brideshead Revisited* we enter upon the first of the third series of Mr. Waugh's novels—the explicitly and consciously Catholic novels. *Brideshead Revisited* is about religion, but it is about nothing except religion, nor is there any question at all of any other religious truth except that of the Catholic Church. It is in no way a work of apologetics. There is no consideration of the historical and metaphysical evidence for the Catholic claims. A reader who had considered that evidence and rejected it would find nothing in the work to alter his rejection. Indeed he might well find his aversion strengthened, as Charles Ryder's aversion was strengthened right up to the closing pages of the book by the intrusion of Father Mackay into the bedroom of the dying Lord Marchmain. The hostile critic might be repelled by

Marchmain's final penitence—might accuse Mr. Waugh of loading his dice, and might quite legitimately argue that, if Mr. Waugh has shown the Catholic Church to be a much stronger force than is generally thought, then, if false, it is the more evil and the more dangerous. However that may be, the significance of *Brideshead Revisited* is the inescapable strength of the hold of the Church over the members of the Flyte family. It does not make them perfect. Brideshead and Cordelia and Lady Marchmain do not try to escape from it. But Brideshead, being a wooden man, holds his faith in a wooden way, and Lady Marchmain, with her instinct to possess, practises her Catholicism in a possessive way. In Sebastian, religion is triumphant in spite of dipsomania and a life of what from a worldly point of view is complete failure. In Lord Marchmain it triumphs in the end alike over intellectual rejection and a desire to refuse its moral discipline. It is instructive to compare the hard and pitiless mockery with which Mr. Waugh describes the murders committed by his two-dimensional characters, such as Mr. Loveday and Miles Plastic, and his obvious sympathy with those who tried to find an excuse for the failings of a 'real' character like Sebastian Flyte. It is true, of course, that Sebastian's failing was not murder but the comparatively trivial one of drunkenness, but that is not really the point. The point is rather that it is Mr. Waugh's opinion that psychiatrists do evil in the world by denying freedom and destroying all human responsibility. Therefore in a two-dimensional work it is sufficient to expose the psychiatrist for a fool by showing the catastrophes that result from a too cocksure attempt to treat crime merely as a disease and to pontificate too confidently on its cure. He therefore writes in the two dimensions as if free will were absolute and its denial a mere folly. But Mr. Waugh in the three dimensions knows well that, though psychiatrists may be fools, yet freedom, though a reality, is also a mystery. Sebastian is a free agent —yet it is uncertain exactly how his freedom operates in regard to his besetting weakness. His action is sinful if it is

a free action, but how far is it a free action? The rest of the
Brideshead family who take a rigid view do not appear in a
sympathetic light. Cordelia, who takes the most generous
view, is shown as the most attractive. The writer of a
pious tract might have thought it edifying to find in the
Flyte family some evidence of easily discernible superior
virtue. Mr. Graham Greene, if he had drawn the character
of Julia, would certainly have drawn her as unable to escape
alike from the Church and from Charles Ryder. She
would presumably have found the usual end in suicide.
But that is not at all Mr. Waugh's way. To Mr. Waugh the
commands of the Church are hard but not impossible.
When the time comes that the break between Julia and
Charles Ryder has to be made, it is made with pain but
finally—and even Charles Ryder understands and, to a
measure, accepts its inevitability.

The critic, of course, may well ask what good their
Catholicism does to the Flytes. Certainly there is no pretence
that they are better citizens than the average on any normal
neutral test, if such a test there be. Certainly there is no
pretence that even on their own Catholic standards their
life is free from sin, or even more nearly free from sin
than that of non-Catholic companions. Sebastian considers
himself 'far, far worse' than Charles Ryder. Charles Ryder
asks in honest bewilderment and impatience, 'Well, for
Heaven's sake, what is the priest for?'

'There were four of you,' I said, 'Cara didn't know the first thing it was
about, and may or may not have believed it; you knew a bit and didn't
believe a word; Cordelia knew about as much and believed it madly;
only poor Bridey knew and believed, and I thought he made a pretty
poor show when it came to explaining. And people go round saying,
"At least Catholics know what they believe". We had a fair cross-section
tonight. . . '

It is not Mr. Waugh's business as a novelist to give some
crisp, text-book answer to these objections, such as Brideshead would have given. Indeed, Charles Ryder's objec-

tions are not susceptible of answer because he does not ask the right question. He assumes throughout that the point of Father Mackay in his relation to Lord Marchmain, the point of the Church in her relation to the world, must be to bring some benefit to Lord Marchmain and to the world. It does not occur to him that the point of it all is not so much that man should be benefited as that God should be glorified. It is for the apologist to give reasons and to defend the truth of the Church's claims. All that Mr. Waugh, the novelist, is concerned to do is to show the strength of those claims on those who have ever come under their influence—to show, whatever superficial appearances of similarity there may be, how there must inevitably be a sundering difference in every action of life between those to whom life is a religious adventure and those to whom it is not such an adventure.

The challenge of *Brideshead Revisited* is the challenge, fairly thrown down, of Augustine's Two Cities. It is not that all are virtuous within the City of God, but simply that there alone is man's home, that there alone can man be truly man. Brideshead is an interesting character precisely because he is such a bore. To some extent it is, of course, true that in his arguments with Charles Ryder Brideshead is right and Ryder is wrong. What seems to Ryder 'upside down' only seems so because of his own crudity—and that is all there is to it. Yet, of course, though Brideshead gives all the correct text-book answers, though he has lived a life of irreproachable virtue, his is a narrow, arid soul, denied those further graces of poetry and humour and adventure—to say nothing of the mystic vision. He knows all that the text-book can demonstrate—and that is a great deal more than most people know in the modern world—but that is all that he knows. All the cups are filled, but his is a small cup. On the other hand, the trouble with Rex Mottram and his friends, with their concentration on money-making in the City and on winning for themselves political jobs, is not that Mottram is especially wicked but that, as Julia complains, he is 'not all there'. Ignorant of so much and missing so much of what is the purpose of life, he is not fully a man. In the same way Celia Ryder, with her life devoted to the capture of Press notices for her husband's shows, has ceased to be 'all there', and Hooper again is not 'all there' in his turn. Life is not truly lived unless it is lived in meeting in one way or another the challenge of religion.

After *Brideshead Revisited* Mr. Waugh turned to the passing relaxation of *Scott-King's Modern Europe*. *Scott-King's Modern Europe* is a simple, but sad, little *jeu d'esprit*. Scott-King is an old, bachelor, classical schoolmaster at a small public school called Grantchester. He is, as Mr. Waugh puts it, a 'dim' man. He happens to have specialized in the work of an obscure seventeenth-century Neutralian poet, who wrote in the Latin language, called Bellorius. He receives one day an invitation from the Neutralian Government to assist in the tercentenary celebration of Bellorius at Simona in Neutralia, expenses paid. He accepts. Going out to Neutralia, he finds that there is no interest among the people there in Bellorius, but that the celebration has been arranged solely as part of a campaign for re-establishing the international prestige of this overlooked country. Nevertheless he goes through his part in the celebrations—not without some difficulties. But, the celebrations finished, his host, Doctor Fe, falls from power, and neither Neutralians nor British diplomats can be got to take the smallest interest in Scott-King's subsequent fate, nor in any way to help him to get the necessary papers to escape from the country and to return to England. Eventually he is smuggled out of the country, and, after humiliating sufferings on a Greek ship, the details of which are kept from us, he turns up in Palestine as an illegal immigrant, where he is lucky enough to run across one of his old pupils. Thus he is able to get back to Grantchester in time for the next term.

Mr. Scott-King is one of the company of William Boot,

that company of quiet people who are only anxious to be left alone but who get caught up to serve the purposes of the vast machines of the modern world—whether they be Governments or newspapers—get caught up to serve their purposes and ruthlessly dropped the moment that the purpose is served. The work is admittedly an extravaganza. It is hard to believe that any visitor would be treated as heartlessly as Mr. Scott-King was treated by the Neutralians and impossible to believe that, if he were so treated, he would be as callously abandoned by the British diplomats. Yet, though an exaggeration, it is an exaggeration *à propos*, and the contrast between Mr. Scott-King's terrifying sufferings and the comic misadventures of William Boot are examples of the hardening of the world, in Mr. Waugh's judgement, between the pre-war days, when the going was good, and the modern life of the ruthless totalitarian tyranny of Government-controlled travel, and of the inextricable complexity of regulation before which the private man despairs.

A casual reader might be tempted also to say of *The Loved One* that it is a *jeu d'esprit* and an extravaganza, but he would be wrong. It is not an extravaganza because, as I understand, the Whispering Glades, whither the human Loved Ones are taken to their last non-denominational resting-place, is in no way an exaggeration of the real mortuary home in Southern California which inspired it. It is true that Denis Barlow, the English secretary of the Happy Hunting Grounds (the home for dead animals), the wooer of Miss Thanatogenos, is, like so many of Mr. Waugh's creations, if we consider him as a real person—consider his gruesome flippancy over the suicide first of Sir Francis Hinsley and later of his fiancée—a very repulsive young man. But, so long as we are in little danger of considering him as in that sense real, we can afford merely to be amused at his flippancies. They, though they carry the story along, are not the real point of the book. The point of the book, if we retranslate it from fiction into propositions, is the study of the attitude of the modern, irreligious man towards death, and as such it is far from a *jeu d'esprit* but rather one of the most serious of all Mr. Waugh's works. Christianity is essentially a religion of death and of life through death. It is the fate of an immortal soul which alone ultimately matters, and that fate is dependent on the condition in which we die. The condition at death is of supreme importance and all life is but a preparation for death. Therefore Christian tradition has always attached an awful solemnity and a supreme dignity to death. The sentimentality which, without any evidence, claims to rob death of all its terrors, eliminates all notion of a judgement, seeks to comfort the living by in every absurd way minimizing the gulf that separates dead from living, is alike worthy of contempt and worthy of satire, and it is that contempt and that satire which Mr. Waugh gives us with his picture of Loved Ones and Waiting Ones, mortuary hostesses and Before Need Arrangements, the death-smile, the Isle of Innisfree, and the artificial dickies.

The prayer of the non-sectarian clergyman over the dead dog: 'Dog that is born of bitch hath but a short time to live, and is full of misery. He cometh up and is cut down like a flower; he fleeth as it were a shadow, and never continueth in one stay . . .'; Dennis Barlow's own advertisement, when he proposes to set up himself as a non-sectarian clergyman: 'Squadron-Leader the Rev. Dennis Barlow begs to announce that he is shortly starting business at 1154 Arbuckle Avenue, Los Angeles. All non-sectarian services expeditiously conducted at competitive prices. Funerals a speciality. Panegyrics in prose or poetry. Confessions heard in strict confidence'—all these are, of course, and are intended to be, excellent fooling, but they are much more than that. The blasphemy is equally intentional. Beneath all the fooling there is the bitter attack on those clowns, who for their commercial purposes and in total ignorance of the whole tradition from which we come, are robbing death and life and the human race of all its dignity. The particular incident which leads Miss Thanatogenos to her suicide is, of course, one of absurd misunderstanding. Mr. Slump, the drunk and sacked author of the column of spiritual direction in the local newspaper, tells Miss Thanatogenos to 'take the elevator to the top floor, find a nice window and jump out' simply in order to get her to stop boring him by her endless telephone conversation while he is trying to drink in his saloon, and the silly girl does it. But her suicide, though immediately accidental, was essentially inevitable. Miss Thanatogenos by nature an ordinary, if silly, girl, could have played a humble, reasonable part in a sane society, in which she was surrounded and sustained by the influence of sane traditions. Mr. Waugh imagines her ancestors in classical Greece as playing such a part. But she wholly lacks the strength to remain sane in an insane world, and before its influences her personality disintegrates. Her death is inevitable because she has forgotten how to live. 'Of course, I never thought her wholly sane, did you?' says Dennis Barlow with characteristically callow insolence, when told of her suicide. But it was not really so much she who was insane as everybody else who was insane. *The Loved One* is a very deep, if somewhat inverted, exposition of the doctine of the Communion of Saints—of the doctrine that most of us can remain human in human company, but that few are strong enough to remain human in a sub-human company.

More direct is the religious statement of *Helena*. In his booklet *The Holy Places*, in which Mr. Waugh utters in powerful and almost perfect prose a passionate protest against what he considers to be a betrayal of the Holy Land in Britain's post-war policy, Mr. Waugh tells us clearly the little that is certainly known and the scraps of surviving legend about St. Helena. All that we know for certain about her is that she was the mother of the Emperor Constantine, and that she is a canonized saint. Tradition ascribes to her the discovery, or, as it is called, the Invention of the True Cross upon which Our Lord was crucified, and rival legends ascribe her birthplace to Drepanum, in what is today Turkey, and to Britain. Mr. Waugh chooses the British version and gives her her birthplace at Colchester, making her the daughter of 'Old King Cole' of the traditional song, or, as he is called in the book, of Coel, Paramount Chief of the Trinovantes. He makes the visiting Constantius of the Imperial family fall in love with her and marry her. Constantius takes her off to his Balkan home at Nish, and eventually, after a series of intrigues and massacres, rises himself to the purple, when for political reasons he divorces her. She lives on quietly at Spalato in the shade of the monstrous palace of the Emperor Diocletian. Then her son, Constantine, tells her that in the renwed turmoil it is necessary for her for her own safety to move to Trèves. She does so. At Spalato her husband, Constantius, had become a devotee of Mithraism, and Helena, confronted with the claims of the Mithraic myths, had asked at once the blunt questions, 'When did these things happen?' and 'Where did they happen?' At Trèves, through the influence of her daughter-in-law, she had come across—particularly in the exposition of her old slave-tutor, Marcias—the similar myths of the new pseudo-mysticism of the Gnostics, the Demiurge, and the Aeon. She asks of Marcias the same questions, 'When did these things happen?' and 'Where did they happen?' From Marcias, as previously from Constantius, she gets no answer save that these are very childish questions, and, getting no answer, she turns to Lactantius, the Christian man of letters, and appeals to him for confirmation that such unsubstantial speculation is 'all bosh, isn't it?'

'All complete bosh, Your Majesty', agrees Lactantius.

She then turns on Lactantius and asks him where and when the mysteries of his religion happened.

'I should say', answers Lactantius, 'that as a man he died two hundred and seventy-eight years ago in the town now called Aelia Capitolina in Palestine.'

'Well that's a straight answer anyway', said Helena.

'How do you know?'—and Lactantius gives her his historical evidences.

So Helena becomes a Christian.

When her son, Constantine, celebrates his jubilee in
Rome, he invites his mother to visit him there. To everyone's surprise she accepts and makes her first visit to the
City. Constantine has, after his victory at the Milvian
Bridge, taken the Christian Church under his patronage,
though he has not himself become a baptized Christian.
Helena finds in Rome a life of appalling intrigue, wicked-
ness, and murder. Constantine, who has already murdered
his father-in-law and most of his relations, now at the
suggestion of his wife Fausta, murders his son, Helena's
grandson, Crispus. At Fausta's suggestion that Helena
herself is involved in the conspiracy against him, Constantine turns on Fausta and has her suffocated in her bath.
Constantine himself, Helena finds, is a megalomaniac—
a triumph, as she puts it, of Power without Grace—victim
of a sort of religion in which it is very difficult to discover
either what is his belief about Christ or what is his belief
about himself; half inclined, it seems, to think of himself
as a god, and conducting personally absurd prayers,
which consist mainly of boasting self-praise. The only
sympathetic, and indeed the only sane, person, whom
Helena meets in Rome—unless we except her grandson,
Crispus—is the old Pope, Sylvester. Mr. Waugh is at his
very high best in the dialogue between what he calls 'these
two admirable old people'.

'The Church isn't a cult for a few heroes. It is the whole
of fallen mankind redeemed. And of course, just at the
moment we're getting a lot of rather shady characters
rolling in, to be on the winning side', says the Pope.

'What do they believe, these shady characters? What
goes on in their minds?' asks Helena.

'God alone knows.'

'It's the one question I've been asking all my life', said
Helena. 'I can't get a straight answer even here in Rome.'

And then after further talk, Helena suddenly asks:

'Where *is* the cross, anyway?'

'What cross, my dear?'

'The only one, the real one.'

'I don't know—I don't think anyone knows. I don't think anyone has ever asked before.'

'It must be somewhere. Wood doesn't just melt like snow. It's not three hundred years old.'

And so Helena accepts it as her special vocation from God to fortify the Church's claim that Christianity is an historical religion in contrast to the mythological religions by which it is surrounded, by discovering the True Cross. She goes to Jerusalem for this purpose. She makes a nuisance of herself. She has apparently failed in her quest, when there appears to her in a dream the Wandering Jew, who, three centuries before, had moved on from his doorstep Our Lord on his way to His crucifixion and had been bidden for his roughness to 'tarry till I come'. He alone is the survivor of those days. He alone knows where the Cross was thrown—into an old underground cistern. The next day Helena makes the men dig in that place, and there behind an old walled-up door they find the three crosses— Our Lord's and those of the two thieves, and also the inscription in the three languages which Pilate put over the Cross of Christ.

There is a number of questions which the book *Helena* raises. The scholar may perhaps, for all I know, question this or that detail of furniture of the scene or of historical description. Into whatever controversies there may be of that nature, I am not competent to enter. The literary critic may question the dignity of one or two touches—such as Lactantius' fear that one day an historian of the Christian story may arise who is devoid of grace, and the comment that his eye then fell upon 'a gibbon' that was playing at his feet. But the real interest of the book is beyond question in the contrat between Helena and the world around her. It is indeed a world, as we are shown it, of

precious little virtue—some rough pagan kindliness in
'Old King Cole', a certain simple soldierly devotion to
duty of the District Commander, the kindliness, it seemed,
of the Illyrian peasants we are shown—but in the world of
what Helena calls 'politics', in the world of those who are
competing for the Imperial posts, there is nothing but
callousness, treachery, murder and madness. It is the
madness which is perhaps most evident, and which most
strikes Helena long before she has come to hate it for
deeper cause. For what sane reason could anyone wish
for this sort of power—this power without grace, which
drives on those who surrender to the pursuit, like a callous
tyranny?

Mr. Waugh does not like politicians. 'In the sixteenth
century,' he writes, 'human life was disordered and
talent stultified by the obsession of theology; to-day we
are plague-stricken by politics.' The politicians who appear
in his pages are not the careful, selfless architects of details
of social legislation. Of politicians of that sort Mr. Waugh
would presumably admit the existence, but they do not
greatly attract his interest. The politicians who appear in
his pages—Rex Mottram in *Brideshead Revisited*, Box-
Bender in *Men At Arms*, Constantius and Constantine in
Helena—are interesting to him as examples of Power without Grace—or perhaps one should rather say, the Roman
politicians are examples of Power without Grace, the
British of self-importance without Grace. Between the
British and the Roman politicians there is naturally the
difference that the British cannot be made to luxuriate in
careless murder with the ease of a Roman Emperor, but,
apart from that, the Romans are important politicians and
the British are unimportant politicians. It is perhaps
necessity rather than choice which has compelled Mr.
Waugh to draw this distinction. One of the difficulties
about the contemporary political novel is that everyone
knows who really was the Prime Minister, what measures
the real Government passed, and the novelist is therefore

compelled to exclude from his pages both events and characters of importance, or else fill them with insubstantial fantasy. But whether he is dealing with important or with unimportant politicians, whatever the precise extravagances to which they resort, Mr. Waugh's lesson is substantially the same. It is that Power, left to itself, tends to corrupt. He who wields Power can only hope to preserve himself from corruption if, like Sylvester, he is constantly conscious that he holds it only as the Vice-Gerent of God and asks continually for Grace to save him from the natural consequences of Power. All forms of Power are dangerous, but self-importance, which masquerades as Power, is supremely ridiculous. Constantine has at least Power. When he says that someone is to be killed, he is killed, but Rex Mottram is simply a loud voice. He does not influence events; he merely pontificates about them, absurdly—and is washed into jobs. Power which makes clever men wicked, makes stupid men stupider. It is the emptiness of the graceless Self-Impotant Man which Mr. Waugh finds so ridiculous, and the politician is more ridiculous than other men because he receives more publicity.

The essence of Constantine's world is that it is a world without grace but it is by no means a world without religion. Whatever service the mythological religions may have rendered in pre-Christian days by preparing men's minds for the Christian revelation, teaching in a vague, half-guessed-at, shadowy way, 'This is how things must be', until the Christian history came to reassure men that 'this is how things are', they are are by Helena's time but an obstacle. Whatever grace God may offer to those who honestly seek Him while in invincible ignorance of His truth, there is no grace in these pundits of the cults. It is a graceless world, though a religious world, and it is a graceless world because it is, as Helena puts it, a world of 'bosh'. The effect cannot be greater than the cause, and religions which can offer no title-deeds of where and when they proved themselves, cannot be strong enough to make men wish to master their desires, and those who do not wish for grace cannot receive it.

There is, in Helena's world, a clear cut between Christianity and other religions and philosophies. There is no such clear cut between all who call themselves Christians and the rest of the world. There are those, like Fausta, who call themselves Christians because it is now fashionable to do so—like Eusebius, because it is politically expedient. There are those from the East who delight in metaphysical subtleties as a mere amusement, and the mark of all these is that, like Arius, they overlook the historical claim of Christianity and try to turn it into a purely metaphysical and mythological religion, and, doing so, they defend themselves of course, as fools have done in all ages, by patter about their sophistication and about the simplicity of their cruder ancestors.

Against this, Helena stands out with the simple answer. 'These things happened. They happened here. They happened on this cross.' She has no more illusion than old Pope Sylvester about the use that people will make even of truth. 'What will they believe in a thousand years' time?' asks the Pope.

The Wandering Jew, an incense-merchant, and therefore tolerant of all religions, since all religions are good for trade, offers her his knowledge for nothing.

'I wouldn't take anything from you, lady, for a little service like that. I shall get paid all right, in time. You have to take a long view in my business. How I see it, this new religion of the Galilean may be in for quite a run. A religion starts, no one knows how. Soon you get holy men and holy places springing up everywhere, old shrines change their names, there's apparitions and pilgrimages. There'll be ladies wanting other things besides the cross. All one wants is to get the thing started properly. One wants a few genuine relics in thoroughly respectable hands. Then everyone else will follow. There won't be enough genuine stuff to meet the demand. That will be my turn. I shall get paid. I wouldn't take anything from you now lady. Glad to see you have the cross. It won't cost you a thing.'

Helena listened and in her mind saw, clear as all else on that brilliant timeless morning, what was in store. She saw the sanctuaries of Christendom become a fair ground, stalls hung with beads and medals, substances yet unknown pressed into sacred emblems; heard a chatter of haggling in tongues yet unspoken. She saw the treasuries of the Church filled with forgeries and impostures. She saw Christians fighting and stealing to get possession of trash. She saw all this, considered it and said:

'It's a stiff price'; and then: 'Show me the cross.'

The third of what might be called the fully Catholic novels is the trilogy, *The Sword of Honour*, which consists of the three novels: *Men At Arms, Officers and Gentlemen* and *Unconditional Surrender*. Guy Crouchback is the last member of an old Catholic family. Deserted by his wife, he is, in *Men At Arms*, living alone in Italy at the outbreak of the war, doing nothing in particular. The Nazi-Soviet Pact, which to so many Englishmen was a cause of confusion, was to him a providential clarification of the issue. The line was at last drawn clear between right and wrong. He returns to England, filled with an enthusiasm to do his bit. At first he meets with nothing but discouragement, but eventually is able to obtain a commission in the Halberdiers. Though in no way remarkable as an officer, though by every external test a 'dim' man, Guy yet has an intense pride in the traditions of the Halberdiers—a pride which survives through all the ups and downs of military life. The book leaves him on a flying-boat returning from Dakar to England to face a court-martial because he had taken part in an unauthorized foray on the mainland of Africa at the bidding of his lunatic brigadier, Ritchie-Hook, and in even deeper disgrace because he had taken a bottle of whisky to his comrade, Apthorpe, in hospital and perhaps caused his death. It is evident enough on every page that this book has been written and published after the war and that Mr. Waugh has been able to use his satiric gifts on the absurdities of some of our measures of security and military precautions in a way that was impossible in *Put Out More Flags*.

Ritchie-Hook with his 'biffing' and Apthorpe with his thunder-box are richly comic characters. The only sorrow is that Apthorpe was killed in this volume and thus was not able to appear in the sequels. But the meat of the book is the study of the character of Guy Crouchback. As a foil to Guy we are given his father, in whom we are intended to see a wholly admirable charater, teaching Greek in his old age at an evacuated preparatory school, living his full Catholic life in a humble, unassuming fashion. Somehow— it is hard to say why—the character is not wholly convincing. In contrast to his father, Guy is a wholly regular and orthodox Catholic, but of an arid, text-book sort and with little personality. There is in him more than an echo of Lord Brideshead, and there is indeed something of the Brideshead touch in his supreme gaucherie. An old schoolmaster with a passion for Catholic genealogy happens to tell him the anecdote of a Catholic who had been deserted by his wife but who afterwards had a child by that wife, although the marriage had civilly come to an end and she was in the eyes of the State and the world the wife of another man. There was no sin in it, says the schoolmaster. How could there be? The idea put into his head, Guy rushes off to London, gets hold of his former wife—a lady of easy virtue who has had three subsequent husbands—and is proceeding to seduce her with prospect of success, when she learns by chance of the technical reason why he had preferred her to another lady, and she leaves him in insulted fury. Characteristically he accepts his rebuff and seems to have no further need for sexual life. *Men At Arms* was followed by *Officers and Gentlemen*. In *Officers and Gentlemen* we get incidentally, as it were, a shot-back or two to Guy Crouchback's father, still continuing in his humble, edifying round as usher at the Catholic preparatory school in the West Country, but the book is not at all directly concerned with a Catholic theme. Indeed the only direct religious experience, if it can be so called, which Guy Crouchback receives in the book is when in Alexandria he goes to confession to a priest whom from his questioning after absolution he suspects—as it turns out, rightly—of being a spy. The book is mainly concerned, as the title implies, with a study of how gentlemen behave before the challenge of modern war. Guy Crouchback joins a company of aristocratic commandos. There are some hilariously funny chapters of pure farce about their training experiences on the West Scottish island of Mugg. Thence they are sent via the Cape to Egypt and from Egypt to Crete just as the rest of the British forces are evacuating that island in total disorder. There are some very vivid chapters, obviously written from personal experience, descriptive of defeat and evacuation. 'The officer and gentleman' does not come very well out of the story. Ivor Claire, in whom Guy had thought that he recognized the perfect example of the type, behaves badly at the evacuation, deserting his men in order to save himself. While the British forces are meeting catastrophe in Crete, an absurd ex-barber, named alternatively Trimmer and McTavish, is winning for himself enormous fame as a democratic hero owing to the fact that he raided France by pure mistake and his men blew up a railway line. He is helped in his publicity by a peer of left-wing opinions, an ex-sporting journalist, Ian Kilbannock. *Men At Arms* had begun with Guy Crouchback's recognition of the Allied cause as a holy cause when he discovered that the Nazis and the Soviets were united in pact in opposition to it. *Officers and Gentlemen* ends with Guy's depression on learning of the Nazi invasion of Russia. While others around welcome this on purely opportunist grounds, to Guy it means the end of any possibility of finding meaning in the war with evil, as is now the case, embattled upon both sides.

The third of the trilogy—*Unconditional Surrender*—appeared later in 1961. (For a time Mr. Waugh thought that the two volumes had exhausted all that he wished to say on the topic.) It depicts the total decline of English standards which resulted from the nation's abandonment of principle in the closing years of the War. In the older generation alone

is there to be found virtue and any full conception of what
life is about. In the early chapters the death of Guy Crouchback's father is described, and we are given a detailed and
moving description of the ceremonies of his funeral, written
with great care and dignity. Guy Crouchback believes, and
we are invited to believe, that the old man was the one
really good person whom Guy had ever known. With his
death a last relic of decency has gone from the world.
There remains of the older generation only Guy's uncle,
Peregrine, himself possessed too of the ancient dignity but,
we are told, a man of less ample personality than his
brother. For the rest the stage is filled with a host of motley
adventurers too ignorant of life to know what they are ad-
venturing about, a gang, to borrow the phrase used by Rex
Mottram in *Brideshead Revisited*, of whom all that one can
say is that they are 'not all there'. There is Guy Crouchback's
wife who returns to him and becomes a Catholic simply
because she has got herself put in the family way by the
barber, Trimmer, whom she loathes and has failed to find a
doctor who would perform for her an abortion. She wants
Guy's money which he has inherited from his father and his
name to give her child. She eventually, along with Guy's
uncle Peregrine, gets killed by a doodlebug. There is a
collection of bizarre bogus officers, most of them British,
one an American, some literary spongers, a Negro doctor
who practises sorcery for a Ministry, disreputable adveturers
from Guy's Cretan past. He is eventually sent out to
Yugoslavia to co-operate with the partisans there. He finds
himself everywhere in the company of people with no roots,
no understanding of what life is about, no sense of the
dignity of its purpose. They have all adopted left-wing
opinions since such opinions are now in fashion and to the
advantage of one's career. Adopting such opinions they have
surrendered to a total callousness to the appalling barbarities
that are being committed in the name of these principles.
Guy, no longer able to find any honourable cause in the
Allied war, loses all wish for life but somehow manages to

survive the war and—we are given to believe—is after it leading a quieter and more contented life with a second wife in the country. The third book of the trilogy is required by the logic of Mr. Waugh's disillusion with the post-war world. It leaves us with a picture of the world in which one institution alone—the Catholic Church—remains in protest against the nihilistic pointlessness of the modern age, and of course the Catholic Church in the world of Crouchback utters its protest in accents somewhat different from those that have been employed by some spokesmen of the Church in this new age of *aggiornamento*. It is a Church in protest against the age, not a Church that seeks in any way to accommodate itself to the age.

After *Men At Arms*, Mr. Waugh's next production was a little *jeu d'esprit*, entitled *Love Among The Ruins*. It is only some half-hour's reading and does not ask to be taken too seriously. It is one of those pessimistic pictures of our future that are now in fashion, but Mr. Waugh does not work out his future with the detail of an Aldous Huxley or a George Orwell. Where George Orwell insists on the dehumanizing effect of absolute power on the ruler, Mr. Waugh insists on its effect on the ruled. Logically enough, in a world of complete boredom, the most popular of all the social services is that of euthanasia. It is only in the times of national calamity, when the people have some bad news to occupy their minds, that they can take any interest in life and that temporarily the demand for euthanasia ceases to outrun the supply.

Just as Scott-King, the pawn and victim of those masters of modern life who have wholly lost all respect for personality, after a manner recalls William Boot—but a William Boot transferred into a less genial, more evil post-war world —so Miles Plastic after a manner recalls Mr. Loveday with his little outing, with his maniac murder of an innocent girl and the repetition of that murder. But there are pleasant traits in Mr. Loveday and the story is too light and fantastic to arouse the horror which his exploits would arouse in real life. There are no pleasant traits in Miles Plastic. Mr. Loveday is a madman. Miles Plastic is a sub-man. He is no longer man.

It is an oddity of Mr. Waugh's work that almost all his principal characters have one parent living, but none of them have two. Paul Pennyfeather, it is true, is an exception in the one direction. He has no more than a guardian. So, too, is William Boot with his uncles, but after him trail a large company of the single-parented. Of these, John Beaver, Basil Seal, and Lord Pastmaster have indeed mothers. But Lady Metroland is only incidentally a mother, Lady Seal, a character of minor importance in *Black Mischief*, and Mrs. Beaver, in *A Handful of Dust*, a character whose baseness is lightly sketched. What Mr. Waugh prefers for his characters is a widower father, eccentric, cynical, Tory, anti-clerical, amusing and uninterested in his parental responsibilities. Between these eccentric characters there is a distinct family resemblance. The fathers of John Plant in *Work Suspended* and Charles Ryder in *Brideshead Revisited* are indeed—doubtless designedly—practically the same characters over again. Nina Blount's old father in *Vile Bodies*, though somewhat odder, is of the same gallery, as indeed, if we move back seventeen hundred years, is Old King Cole, the father of St. Helena, though it is true that he was fortified against the austerities of widowerhood not only by three fiddlers but also by three mistresses. Mr. Waugh has clearly a marked aversion to the depiction of his characters as the children of two regular and living parents. He tries in *Men At Arms* to give us a portrait of another type of parent, Guy Crouchback's widower father—admirable, pious, modest, unselfish—but the attempt is not altogether sucessful, though he warms more to the task with the two later volumes of the trilogy. But Mr. Waugh can manage erratic parents better. Of all his main characters the Flytes alone have two parents living, when the book begins, and they are not living together, nor can the Marchmains be held up as an example of normal domesticity.

Now this repetition in character after character and book after book of an incomplete family background is clearly no accident. The family is the essential unit of society. He who comes into life from a broken or incomplete family comes into life to that extent an incomplete man, and modern society, as Mr. Waugh sees it, whether he be looking at it in his three-dimensional or in his two-dimensional novels, whether he be engaged in pointing a Catholic contrast to secular futility or merely in exposing futility, is essentially a society of incomplete men and women: a society of men and women who, having renounced the religion for which they were born, are losing rapidly the culture that is based on that religion and the humanity that is based on that culture. I have selected as a turning-point in Mr. Waugh's literary, intellectual, and artistic development, his study of Edmund Campion in 1935, and from that study he learnt not so much the truth of the Catholic religion, which he had already accepted a few years before, but rather what he perhaps feels more intensely than some other Catholic apologists—the sundering nature of its claims.

In 1957 Mr. Waugh published *The Ordeal of Gilbert Pinfold*, a book wholly different in kind from any other he has written. Confessedly almost autobiographical, it is the account of a voyage taken to Ceylon by a successful middle-aged novelist who is ill because he has consumed the wrong sort of sleeping draught. He is assailed by voices which threaten him and make obscene suggestions to him. The book opens with a chapter of ruthlessly searching autobiographical analysis, in the form of an analysis of the character of Gilbert Pinfold, and many readers have found these the most interesting chapters in the book. Some have professed to find the chapters of near-madness amusing. It is true that the suggestions of the voices are often ridiculous enough and some of Pinfold's remarks to his fellow-passengers are comical in themselves, but a reader has to be hard-boiled indeed who finds madness funny. Eventually, on his return to London, Pinfold is able to drive off the voices by recognising that they are imaginary and by telling them so. The tale is powerfully told. What remains odd is that one who has been through such experiences should be willing to tell the world of them in such a comparatively casual fashion, and, as it were, to lunch out on them.

Mr. Waugh had always a high admiration for the work of Monsignor Ronald Knox, whom he thought to be the greatest master of English prose of our time. In 1949 he made a selected collection of Monsignor Knox's sermons and published them with an introduction by himself. On Monsignor Knox's death in September, 1957, Mr. Waugh was left as his literary executor and undertook the task of writing his life. The work appeared in 1959. It was universally hailed as a masterly piece of prose. Never had Mr. Waugh's writing been more careful and more triumphant. But there were some critics and some friends of Monsignor Knox who felt that it made him appear more misanthropic and low-spirited than was warranted by the facts. It is certainly true that Monsignor Knox, like most great humorists, had in him a vein of melancholy. Few can bear the awful strain of being expected to say witty things all the time, and humorists—and particularly intellectual humorists —require to retire at times into solitude or into the company of a few intimate friends and into a world where there are no jokes. Monsignor Knox most certainly had that strain in his character, but he was also a man who greatly loved and was most greatly loved and there were some who felt that Mr. Waugh, by almost insisting on his low spirits, transferred to the subject some of the qualities of the biographer, as biographers sometimes do. All biographies are in a sense autobiographies. Others felt that Monsignor Knox's literary difficulties with the hierarchy were perhaps a little more ruthlessly exposed than he with his exquisite delicacy and humility would have wished. Besides Mr. Waugh frankly wrote of him as a friend and as a literary man. He specifically did not profess to hold the key to the secret of his spiritual life.

Yet, with such reservations fairly made, none can challenge the verdict that is this one of the most distinguished biographies of our time.

More recently Mr. Waugh has settled down to the task of writing his autobiography. The first volume, *A Little Learning*, has already appeared and the second volume will appear shortly. The first volume only carries his life up to the time of his assistant mastership in North Wales immediately after he had gone down from Oxford. There is an attractive tribute to his parents and those who were his friends at Oxford will be grateful for the kindly things that they find said about them. But Mr. Waugh had not by that age begun to develop interest in those topics which were to dominate his mind in later years, and therefore the later volumes of the autobiography will almost certainly prove more interesting than this first beginning.

EVELYN WAUGH

A Select Bibliography

(Books published in London, unless otherwise stated)

Collected Editions:

WHEN THE GOING WAS GOOD (1946). *Travel*
From *Labels, Remote People, Ninety-two Days,* and *Waugh in Abyssinia.*

UNIFORM EDITION OF THE NOVELS, up to and including *Brideshead Revisited* (1947-9); also *Helena* (1957).

Separate Works:

P.R.B.: an Essay on the pre-Raphaelite Brotherhood 1847-1854 (1926)
—only 25 copies were printed.

ROSSETTI (1928). *Biography*

DECLINE AND FALL (1928) *Novel*

VILE BODIES (1930) *Novel*
—dramatic version by H. D. Bradley, 1931.

LABELS (1930). *Travel*

REMOTE PEOPLE (1931). *Travel*

BLACK MISCHIEF (1932). *Novel*

NINETY-TWO DAYS (1934). *Travel*

EDMUND CAMPION (1935). *Biography*

MR. LOVEDAY'S LITTLE OUTING (1936). *Stories*

WAUGH IN ABYSSINIA (1936). *Travel*

A HANDFUL OF DUST (1937). *Novel*

SCOOP (1938). *Novel*

ROBBERY UNDER LAW (1939). *Commentary*

PUT OUT MORE FLAGS (1942). *Novel*

WORK SUSPENDED (1942). *Unfinished Novel*
—first published in a limited edition: reprinted 1949, in slightly amended form, together with stories including 'Mr. Loveday's Little Outing'.

BRIDESHEAD REVISITED (1945). *Novel*

SCOTT-KING'S MODERN EUROPE (1947). *Novel*

THE LOVED ONE (1948). *Novel*

HELENA (1950). *Novel*

MEN AT ARMS (1952). *Novel*
—the first volume of a war trilogy.

LOVE AMONG THE RUINS (1953). *Novel*

THE HOLY PLACES (1953). *Travel*

OFFICERS AND GENTLEMEN (1955). *Novel*
—the second volume of a war trilogy.

THE ORDEAL OF GILBERT PINFOLD (1957). *Narrative*

THE LIFE OF THE RIGHT REVEREND RONALD KNOX (1959). *Biography*

UNCONDITIONAL SURRENDER (1961). *Novel*
—the third volume of a war trilogy.

A LITTLE LEARNING (1964)
—the first volume of an autobiography.

THE SWORD OF HONOUR (1965).
—a final version of *Men at Arms, Officers and Gentlemen* and *Unconditional Surrender*.

Some Critical Studies

MARIA CROSS by D. O'Donnell (C. C. O'Brien) (1953).
—contains a chapter on Waugh.

EVELYN WAUGH: PORTRAIT OF AN ARTIST by F. J. Stepp (1958).

EVELYN WAUGH by M. Bradbury (1964).

WRITERS AND THEIR WORK

General Editor: GEOFFREY BULLOUGH

The first 55 issues in the Series appeared under the General Editorship of T. O. BEACHCROFT
Issues 56-169 appeared under the General Editorship of BONAMY DOBRÉE

General Surveys:

THE DETECTIVE STORY IN BRITAIN:
Julian Symons
THE ENGLISH BIBLE: Donald Coggan
ENGLISH VERSE EPIGRAM:
G. Rostrevor Hamilton
ENGLISH HYMNS: A. Pollard
ENGLISH MARITIME WRITING:
Hakluyt to Cook: Oliver Warner
THE ENGLISH SHORT STORY I: & II:
T. O. Beachcroft
ENGLISH SERMONS: Arthur Pollard
ENGLISH TRAVELLERS IN THE
NEAR EAST: Robin Fedden
THREE WOMEN DIARISTS: M. Willy

Sixteenth Century and Earlier:

FRANCIS BACON: J. Max Patrick
CHAUCER: Nevill Coghill
LANGLAND: Nevill Coghill
MALORY: M. C. Bradbrook
MARLOWE: Philip Henderson
MORE: E. E. Reynolds
RALEGH: Agnes Latham
SIDNEY: Kenneth Muir
SKELTON: Peter Green
SPENSER: Rosemary Freeman
WYATT: Sergio Baldi

Seventeenth Century:

SIR THOMAS BROWNE: Peter Green
BUNYAN: Henri Talon
CAVALIER POETS: Robin Skelton
CONGREVE: Bonamy Dobrée
DONNE: F. Kermode
DRYDEN: Bonamy Dobrée
ENGLISH DIARISTS: Evelyn and
Pepys: Margaret Willy
JOHN FORD: Clifford Leech
GEORGE HERBERT: T. S. Eliot
HERRICK: John Press
HOBBES: T. E. Jessop
BEN JONSON: J. B. Bamborough
LOCKE: Maurice Cranston
ANDREW MARVELL: John Press
MILTON: E. M. W. Tillyard
RESTORATION COURT POETS:
V. de S. Pinto
SHAKESPEARE: C. J. Sisson
SHAKESPEARE:
CHRONICLES: Clifford Leech
EARLY COMEDIES: Derek Traversi
FINAL PLAYS: Frank Kermode

GREAT TRAGEDIES: Kenneth Muir
HISTORIES: L. C. Knights
LATER COMEDIES: G. K. Hunter
POEMS: F. T. Prince
PROBLEM PLAYS: Peter Ure
ROMAN PLAYS: T. J. B. Spencer
THREE METAPHYSICAL POETS:
Margaret Willy
IZAAK WALTON: Margaret Bottrall
WEBSTER: Ian Scott-Kilvert
WYCHERLEY: P. F. Vernon

Eighteenth Century:

BERKELEY: T. E. Jessop
BLAKE: Kathleen Raine
BOSWELL: P. A. W. Collins
BURKE: T. E. Utley
BURNS: David Daiches
WM. COLLINS: Oswald Doughty
COWPER: N. Nicholson
CRABBE: R. L. Brett
DEFOE: J. R. Sutherland
FIELDING: John Butt
GAY: Oliver Warner
GIBBON: C. V. Wedgwood
GOLDSMITH: A. Norman Jeffares
GRAY: R. W. Ketton-Cremer
HUME: Montgomery Belgion
JOHNSON: S. C. Roberts
POPE: Ian Jack
RICHARDSON: R. F. Brissenden
SHERIDAN: W. A. Darlington
CHRISTOPHER SMART: G. Grigson
SMOLLETT: Laurence Brander
STEELE AND ADDISON:
A. R. Humphreys
STERNE: D. W. Jefferson
SWIFT: J. Middleton Murry
HORACE WALPOLE: Hugh Honour

Nineteenth Century:

MATTHEW ARNOLD: Kenneth Allott
JANE AUSTEN: S. Townsend Warner
BAGEHOT: N. St. John-Stevas
THE BRONTË SISTERS: P. Bentley
BROWNING: John Bryson
ELIZABETH BARRETT BROWNING:
Alethea Hayter
SAMUEL BUTLER: G. D. H. Cole
BYRON: Herbert Read
CARLYLE: David Gascoyne
LEWIS CARROLL: Derek Hudson
CLOUGH: Isobel Armstrong

COLERIDGE: Kathleen Raine
DE QUINCEY: Hugh Sykes Davies
DICKENS: K. J. Fielding
DISRAELI: Paul Bloomfield
GEORGE ELIOT: Lettice Cooper
SUSAN FERRIER & JOHN GALT:
                     W. M. Parker
FITZGERALD: Joanna Richardson
MRS. GASKELL: Miriam Allott
GISSING: A. C. Ward
THOMAS HARDY: R. A. Scott-James
             and C. Day Lewis
HAZLITT: J. B. Priestley
HOOD: Laurence Brander
G. M. HOPKINS: Geoffrey Grigson
T. H. HUXLEY: William Irvine
KEATS: Edmund Blunden
LAMB: Edmund Blunden
LANDOR: G. Rostrevor Hamilton
EDWARD LEAR: Joanna Richardson
MACAULAY: G. R. Potter
MEREDITH: Phyllis Bartlett
JOHN STUART MILL: M. Cranston
WILLIAM MORRIS: P. Henderson
NEWMAN: J. M. Cameron
PATER: Iain Fletcher
PEACOCK: J. I. M. Stewart
ROSSETTI: Oswald Doughty
CHRISTINA ROSSETTI:
              Georgina Battiscombe
RUSKIN: Peter Quennell
SIR WALTER SCOTT: Ian Jack
SHELLEY: Stephen Spender
SOUTHEY: Geoffrey Carnall
R. L. STEVENSON: G. B. Stern
SWINBURNE: H. J. C. Grierson
TENNYSON: F. L. Lucas
THACKERAY: Laurence Brander
FRANCIS THOMPSON: P. Butter
TROLLOPE: Hugh Sykes Davies
OSCAR WILDE: James Laver
WORDSWORTH: Helen Darbishire

Twentieth Century:

W. H. AUDEN: Richard Hoggart
HILAIRE BELLOC: Renée Haynes
ARNOLD BENNETT: F. Swinnerton
EDMUND BLUNDEN: Alec M. Hardie
ELIZABETH BOWEN: Jocelyn Brooke
ROBERT BRIDGES: J. Sparrow
ROY CAMPBELL: David Wright
JOYCE CARY: Walter Allen
G. K. CHESTERTON: C. Hollis
WINSTON CHURCHILL: John Connell
R. G. COLLINGWOOD: E.W.F. Tomlin
I. COMPTON-BURNETT:
             Pamela Hansford Johnson

JOSEPH CONRAD: Oliver Warner
WALTER DE LA MARE: K. Hopkins
NORMAN DOUGLAS: Ian Greenlees
T. S. ELIOT: M. C. Bradbrook
FIRBANK & BETJEMAN: J. Brooke
FORD MADOX FORD: Kenneth Young
E. M. FORSTER: Rex Warner
CHRISTOPHER FRY: Derek Stanford
JOHN GALSWORTHY: R. H. Mottram
ROBERT GRAVES: M. Seymour-Smith
GRAHAM GREENE: Francis Wyndham
L. P. HARTLEY & ANTHONY POWELL:
        P. Bloomfield and B. Bergonzi
A. E. HOUSMAN: Ian Scott-Kilvert
ALDOUS HUXLEY: Jocelyn Brooke
HENRY JAMES: Michael Swan
JAMES JOYCE: J. I. M. Stewart
RUDYARD KIPLING: Bonamy Dobrée
D. H. LAWRENCE: Kenneth Young
C. DAY LEWIS: Clifford Dyment
WYNDHAM LEWIS: E. W. F. Tomlin
LOUIS MACNEICE: John Press
KATHERINE MANSFIELD: Ian Gordon
JOHN MASEFIELD: L. A. G. Strong
SOMERSET MAUGHAM: J. Brophy
GEORGE MOORE: A. Norman Jeffares
EDWIN MUIR: J. C. Hall
J. MIDDLETON MURRY: Philip Mairet
GEORGE ORWELL: Tom Hopkinson
POETS OF 1939-45 WAR:
               R. N. Currey
POWYS BROTHERS: R. C. Churchill
J. B. PRIESTLEY: Ivor Brown
HERBERT READ: Francis Berry
FOUR REALIST NOVELISTS:
               Vincent Brome
BERTRAND RUSSELL: Alan Dorward
BERNARD SHAW: A. C. Ward
EDITH SITWELL: John Lehmann
OSBERT SITWELL: Roger Fulford
C. P. SNOW: William Cooper
STRACHEY: R. A. Scott-James
SYNGE & LADY GREGORY:
               E. Coxhead
DYLAN THOMAS: G. S. Fraser
EDWARD THOMAS: Vernon Scannell
G. M. TREVELYAN: J. H. Plumb
WAR POETS: 1914-18: E. Blunden
EVELYN WAUGH: Christopher Hollis
H. G. WELLS: Montgomery Belgion
PATRICK WHITE: R. F. Brissenden
CHARLES WILLIAMS: J. Heath-Stubbs
VIRGINIA WOOLF: B. Blackstone
W. B. YEATS: G. S. Fraser
ANDREW YOUNG & R. S. THOMAS:
             L. Clark and R. G. Thomas